F-22
RAPTORS

BY DENNY VON FINN

EPIC

BELLWETHER MEDIA · MINNEAPOLIS, MN

EPIC BOOKS are no ordinary books. They burst with intense action, high-speed heroics, and shadows of the unknown. Are you ready for an Epic adventure?

This edition first published in 2013 by Bellwether Media, Inc.

No part of this publication may be reproduced in whole or in part without written permission of the publisher. For information regarding permission, write to Bellwether Media, Inc., Attention: Permissions Department, 5357 Penn Avenue South, Minneapolis, MN 55419.

Library of Congress Cataloging-in-Publication Data

Von Finn, Denny.
F-22 Raptors / by Denny Von Finn.
   p. cm. – (Epic books: military vehicles)
Includes bibliographical references and index.
Audience: Ages 6-12.
Summary: "Engaging images accompany information about F-22 Raptors. The combination of high-interest subject matter and light text is intended for students in grades 2 through 7"–Provided by publisher.
ISBN 978-1-60014-817-0 (hbk. : alk. paper)
1. F/A-22 (Jet fighter plane)–Juvenile literature. I. Title.
UG1242.F5V655 2013
623.74'64–dc23   2012002394

Printed in the United States of America, North Mankato, MN.

TABLE OF CONTENTS

F-22 RAPTORS

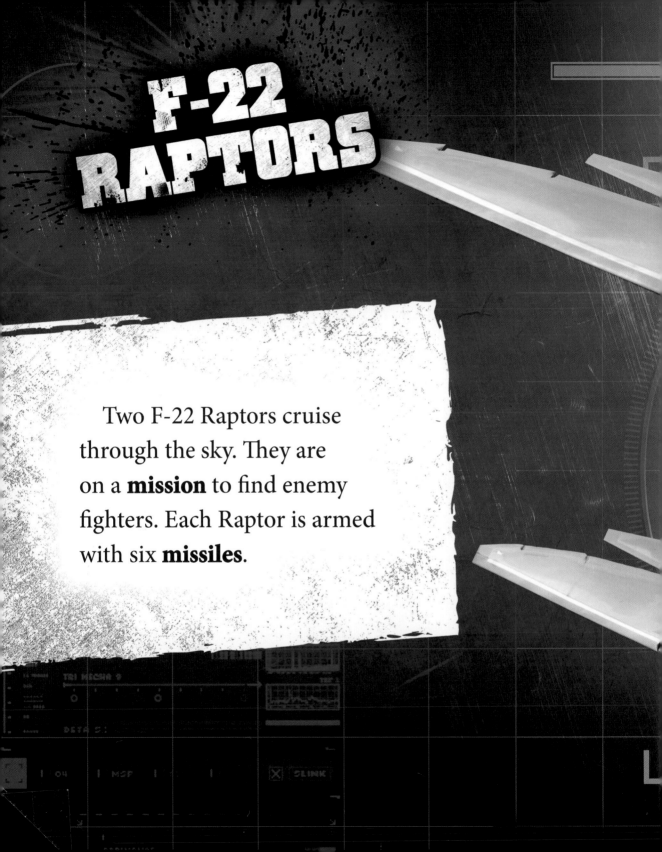

Two F-22 Raptors cruise through the sky. They are on a **mission** to find enemy fighters. Each Raptor is armed with six **missiles**.

The Raptor pilots pick up enemy missiles on **radar**. Both Raptors drop **chaff** to confuse the missiles.

The Raptor pilots now turn toward the enemy fighters. It is their turn to fire!

Raptor Fact

The Raptor can move faster and easier than any other jet fighter in the world.

STEALTH AND WEAPONS

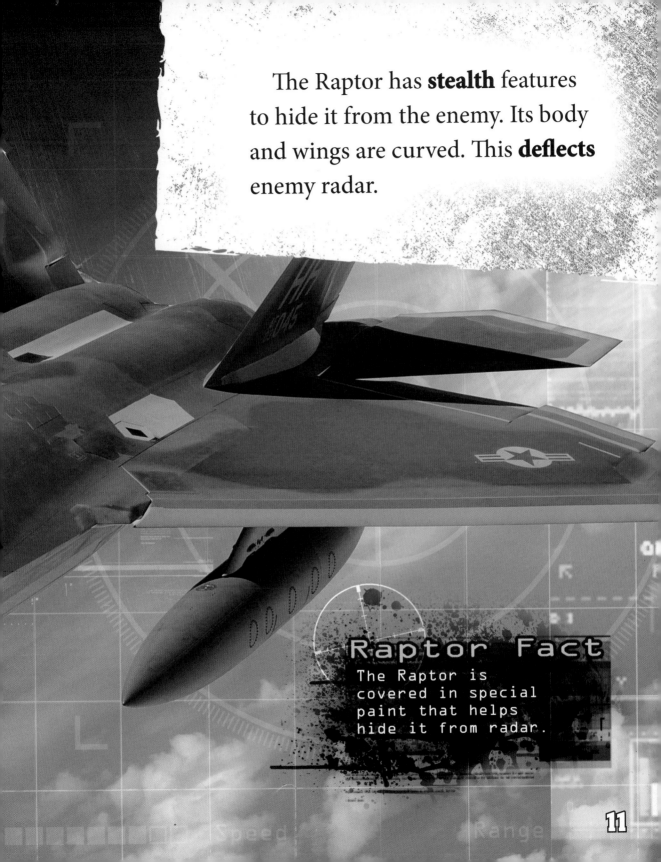

The Raptor has **stealth** features to hide it from the enemy. Its body and wings are curved. This **deflects** enemy radar.

Raptor Fact

The Raptor is covered in special paint that helps hide it from radar.

FINS

The Raptor's two large jet engines give off a lot of heat. Fins hide the hot engines from **heat-seeking weapons**.

The Raptor has bombs, missiles, and a large gun. Missiles and bombs are kept in **weapons bays** during stealth missions.

Raptor Fact

The Raptor's gun can fire up to 6,000 rounds per minute!

WEAPONS BAY

MISSILE

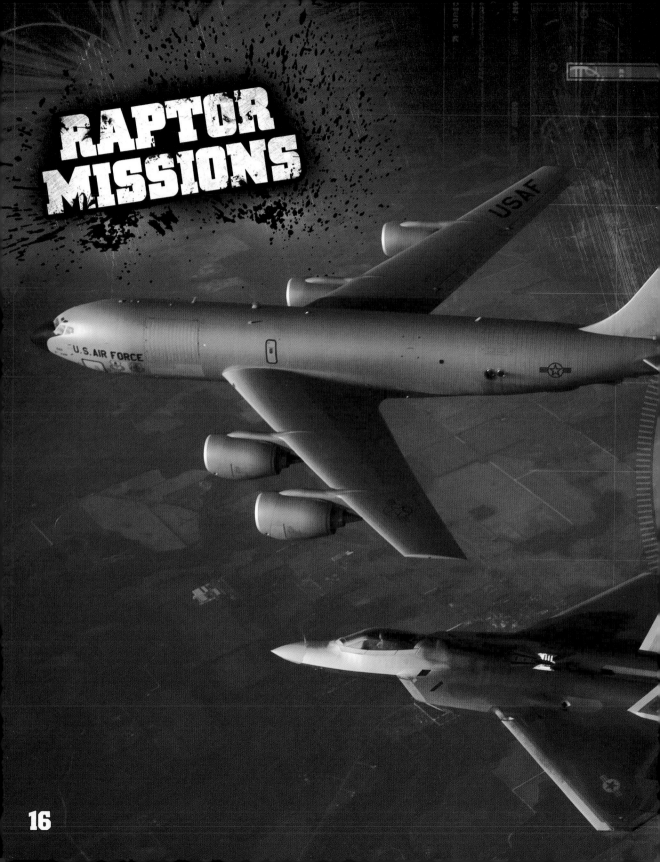

RAPTOR MISSIONS

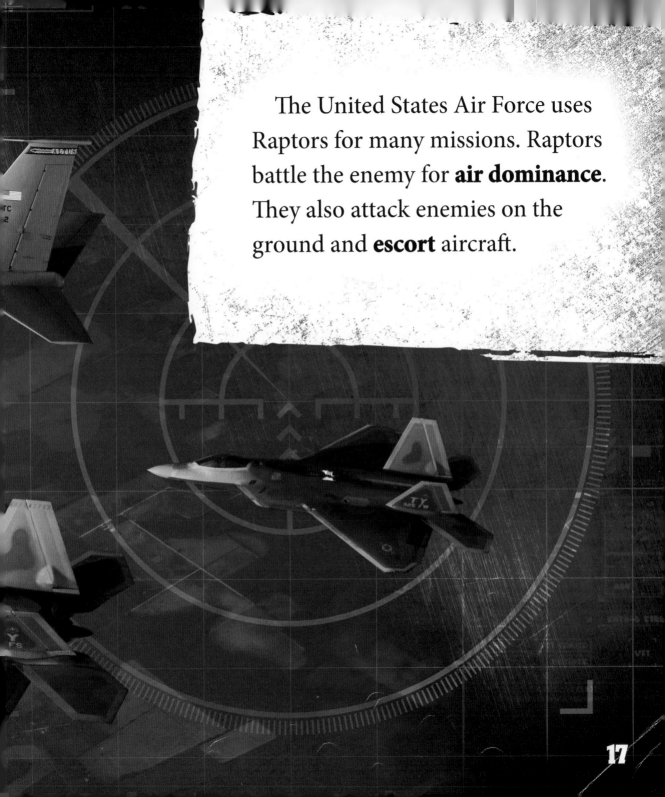

The United States Air Force uses Raptors for many missions. Raptors battle the enemy for **air dominance**. They also attack enemies on the ground and **escort** aircraft.

WINGMATE

Sometimes several Raptors
are sent on a mission. They fly
in **formation** to stay safe and
alert. The **wingmates** protect
the lead Raptor from threats.

VEHICLE BREAKDOWN:
F-22 RAPTOR

Used By:	U.S. Air Force
Entered Service:	2005
Length:	62 feet (18.9 meters)
Height:	16.7 feet (5.1 meters)
Wingspan:	44.5 feet (13.6 meters)
Weight:	60,000 pounds (27,215 kilograms)
Top Speed:	Around 1,520 miles (2,450 kilometers) per hour
Range:	1,840 miles (2,960 kilometers)
Ceiling:	Above 50,000 feet (15,240 meters)
Weapons:	missiles, bombs, gun
Crew:	1
Primary Missions:	air dominance, escorting

The Raptor is one of the most advanced jet fighters. It will dominate the skies for many years to come.

GLOSSARY

air dominance—control of the skies

chaff—objects dropped from an aircraft to confuse enemy weapons

deflects—causes something to scatter

escort—to travel alongside and protect

formation—the pattern in which a group of planes flies

heat-seeking weapons—weapons that follow the heat of objects

missiles—explosives that are guided to a target

mission—a military task

radar—a system that uses radio waves to locate targets

stealth—an aircraft's ability to fly without being spotted by radar

weapons bays—areas inside of a Raptor that hold weapons; the bays open when a weapon is fired.

wingmates—pilots who fly Raptors in support of another Raptor

TO LEARN MORE

At the Library

Bledsoe, Karen and Glen. *Fighter Planes: Fearless Fliers*. Berkeley Heights, N.J.: Enslow Publishers, 2006.

Trumbauer, Lisa. *Fighter Jet*. Chicago, Ill.: Raintree, 2008.

Von Finn, Denny. *Jet Fighters*. Minneapolis, Minn.: Bellwether Media, 2010.

On the Web

Learning more about F-22 Raptors is as easy as 1, 2, 3.

1. Go to www.factsurfer.com.

2. Enter "F-22 Raptors" into the search box.

3. Click the "Surf" button and you will see a list of related Web sites.

With factsurfer.com, finding more information is just a click away.

INDEX